LATENT HEAT

LATENT HEAT

CATHERINE HUNTER

First printing, December 1997
Second printing, August 1998
Third printing, September 2002

Photo of Catherine Hunter by Anne Marie Resta.
Cover art by Caroline Dukes.
Cover design by Terry Gallagher/Doowah Design.
The author thanks George Amabile for invaluable editorial advice and the Manitoba Arts Council for a grant which provided the time to write.

Some of these poems have previously appeared in *CV2*, *Street*, *Windhorse*, and the Winnipeg Art Gallery.

We acknowledge the support of The Canada Council for the Arts for our publishing program.
Printed and bound in Canada by Veilleux Impression à Demande.

Canadian Cataloguing in Publication Data

Hunter, Catherine, 1957–
Latent heat

Poems.
ISBN 0-921833-55-5

I. Title.

PS8565.U5783L38 1997 C811′.54 C98-900006-0
PR1999.3.H255L38 1997

Signature Editions, P.O. Box 206, RPO Corydon Winnipeg, Manitoba, R3M 3S7

Contents

States of Grace
- Vertigo
- Fever
- Poison
- Blindness
- Compulsion
- Nausea
- Delusion
- Sunstroke
- Paralysis
- Hunger
- Delirium
- Deliverance

Rush Hour

Drawing Water

Ghost Stories

Latent Heat
- Seven Arteries
- The Seventh Day
- The Other Side
- The Windowsill
- The Letter L
- The Movie
- 13 Lines in Order to Forget You
- The Twenty-sixth
- January
- Navigation
- Elsewhere
- The First Lesson
- The Naked Eye
- Fainting
- For God So Loved the World
- Opening
- Experts
- Mess
- Gifted
- True North

States of Grace

VERTIGO

Tell me about heaven, I said.
I lay flat on my back in the grass
while the cumulous clouds revolved
in the hot blue sky. In those days
we used to spin ourselves dizzy
on purpose and make up lies
while the whirling slowed and came to rest.
The Catholic boys always had the best stories:
pearls and honey and happy, wingèd creatures
with voices like nightingales. I listened
to all of this while my brother dipped a loop of wire
into a jar of soap suds and blew bubbles.
The Catholic boys stood above me
as they spoke, their blond heads barely
blocking the sun, a single corona of sparks
and diamonds in their hair, and the fat globes
of light were rising, indigo and lavender and ruby
and the world was supposed to stop spinning, eventually,
but it never did. The ground was fluid
under my back, as if I were resting
on that cool bank of clouds and sailing
the circumference of the sky. I was extremely young.
I felt it might be possible to drift through life
very easily, looking down at the neighbourhood
as I passed over it.

Fever

The Catholic boys knew all about hell.
It was like having a fever, they said,
a hundred and two degrees, and that was the place
I was going to end up, if I didn't believe:
a black hole under the ground, where flames
as dark as shadows licked at your eyeballs
and burned the hair right off your head
and not even God could hear you
screaming, or you could get stuck
between this world and the next, forced
to wander homeless and alone.
I asked my mother if all of this was true
and she said, *some people think so.*
She was busy with my brother, who had a case
of meningitis, though I didn't know it
yet. She carried the wet towels
all the way down the stairs in a laundry tub
and wrapped his skinny body like a mummy.
I looked at the pictures in my book about the Buddha
and wondered what he meant by suffering.
After a while, my mother sent me across the street
to play with the Catholic boys.
One of them whispered in my ear, *your brother*
isn't baptized, is he? One of them
tried to kiss me under the stairs.

Poison

The eyes of potatoes were dangerous.
That's what the other kids said.
Also the clear, red berries that grew
in the policeman's hedge. Even the combination
of cucumbers and milk could do you in,
your stomach turning black inside and bursting.
Stinging nettles sprouted by the train tracks
where we set our pennies on the rail
and seeded the ditch with coiled paper flowers
we bought in Chinatown, watching them swell
and bloom like stars until they grew heavy with water.
My mother pushed the baby stroller around and around
the American Consulate downtown, as if she could stop
the nuclear testing with the sheer beauty
of her moving body. Meanwhile at school
the kids stood up beside their desks
and recited the Lord's Prayer, while I stayed quiet
the way my father said I should if I had the guts
to disobey, and apparently I did.
I walked down the backlane where I wasn't allowed
to walk. I was a stubborn girl, and for each
stubborn girl there is a man in the backlane, waiting.
Mine had a dull coil of barbed wire in the back seat
of his car and something in his lap I'd never seen before.
He touched me and I ran, the way I always ran
when the bell sounded for the air-raid drill at school.
We all ran, though we knew we were lucky children.
We were spoiled, my father said, and the war
was merely a rumour to us, an interrupted story
traced in the maze of skin grafts on his face,
the sunken lids that made the other kids stare.
I knew I wasn't going to be strafed by shrapnel
on the way home, but I ran anyway.
I ran past the policeman's hedge with its clear,
red berries, and all of a sudden they looked delicious to me.

I thought that if they were really poison
my mother would have warned me specifically about them.
I thought about eating one, or maybe
a whole handful, just to see the other kids' faces
turning white, but instead I stole a bottle of whisky
and passed it among them. We dared each other to drink
until our bellies grew warm and we giggled and became
unaccountably dizzy and threw up right there
in the backlane where we weren't
supposed to be.

Blindness

None of the other kids in the neighbourhood
would have taken it. They said so themselves.
They came to our yard and climbed the crabapple tree,
screwing up their comical faces with pleasure
as the sour fruit dried up their tongues
and they kept right on talking, none of us knowing then
so many of them would die before their time, and how
could we have known? We couldn't see
into the future, and we didn't know our father
was getting annoyed with the noises we were making.
That was the word he used, *annoyed,* it sent a chill
right through my spine and paralyzed my brother.
Why do you take it? the other kids asked,
he can't even see you. Why don't you just
dodge him and take off? We said nothing
because back then some things were too powerful to say.
Our father came out to the doorway, and the kids
who were willing to risk becoming invisible
ran right past him and escaped.
We wondered which name he would call
and he called my brother. And my brother went.
I crouched in the branches with the two boys
who had stayed behind, and one of them placed his hand
on my back with a pressure that might have been sympathy,
a sort of apology for what was happening or for the way
his own early death was going to wound me to the bone.
The three of us held our breath and pretended
we were not there as we watched my brother take it.
We saw him raise his eyes for a moment, as if for a moment
he'd forgotten who he was, and then we saw him
take it some more.

COMPULSION

The number six was dark like the leaves
of citrus plants, and three was a light
and airy colour, translucent as the pale
green ceiling of the swimming pool in summer.
Sometimes I thought too long about infinity and zero,
the various densities of numbers, their properties
of elasticity. I counted the trees on the boulevard,
the cracks in the cement, the number of times
the ice-cream boy came down the street on a Saturday
afternoon, with his bells and his lethal dry ice.
He said he would put a chunk of it down the front
of my shirt. He said a kid once climbed into the cart,
and the dry ice seared every inch of skin
right off his body. But I held all this at bay.
I touched the streetlights as I passed them by
in the dark, scraping my fingernails against
their peeling, rusted posts. Sometimes on purpose
I'd miss one just to test myself, to see how far I could go
before turning back, to find out just how crazy
I really was. At school sometimes the clock stopped dead
in the middle of day, usually in English class
when the kids were taking turns at stuttering
through the paragraphs in *Wide Open Windows*,
which I had read straight through on the first day
of September, so I counted the bicycles in the bicycle rack
outside, the holes in the ceiling tiles, while I waited
for time to begin again. Or I'd stand on second base
in the playground and wonder why
I had been chosen to be born, why I was the one
whose mind kept moving while everyone else, it seemed,
was getting a rest—oh I was arrogant. I thought
I was different, I thought if only I could
grow up, I could separate myself from them and go
my own way, whatever that might mean, and then

they would all start pitching and running
and yelling with their hoarse voices,
and there I'd be, a kid on second base again, a kid
who could read a little bit faster than most,
someone who couldn't stop counting the trees
and the streetlights and the minutes
that were moving me toward something
I couldn't know about yet and wasn't sure
I wanted.

NAVSEA

I sat in the dentist's office, smelling
the bright needles and the cotton swabs,
and all I could think of was how embarrassed
I was going to be when I fainted again.
I always fainted, even though he never
fixed my teeth. I had perfect teeth
and a weak and cowardly imagination.
I was stuck in the preliminary practices
of dharma and could not move beyond them.
I had no control over my own mind.
Often I thought about the man in the lane
and my stomach quivered below my ribs.
I thought about the time my father sent me
to the eye doctor, and I saw the drawer of eyes
peering out at me, blue ones. They were only
made of glass, of course, and the doctor merely
wanted to look at me because my father's sister
said my eyes were the exact same shade
of blue that his had been before the war.
I tried to focus my thoughts and be free
from stupidity, but I worried that maybe
there was something no one dared to tell me.
Why did I feel so sick when there was nothing
to be sick about? I went to the swimming pool
and dived off the three-meter spring board.
I swam and swam and wouldn't stop
swimming, eighty, ninety, a hundred
lengths of the pool, each crossing counted off
in my head, and every number known to me
exactly, in my gut, the only place
where I knew anything.

Sunstroke

All I could see was the white pain
behind my eyes, and even the shade
beneath the fir trees in the park
was white with heat. I lay there
on the grass and heard the teachers
talk about how pale I was, and I wanted
to crawl away like an animal or be put to sleep.
My mother arrived with her cool hands
and took me home and fed me aspirins, crushed
in honey, and the grit stuck
in my teeth like tiny boulders.
I could no longer tell if things were large
or small. I was floating on razor-wire
above the bed, looking down at the room
through an unreliable telescope. Daylight
would not go away. I had seen too much
I was afraid to tell. I wasn't sure if I could
keep the soldiers out of the bedroom.
That night I stood up straight in my pyjamas
and threw the writing desk against the door.
My mother tried to calm me, but I was too strong,
I was always too strong, and she could only speak
to me in her soft voice while I destroyed everything.

Delusion

After my great grandmother passed away
she came to stand at the foot of my bed
and smiled at me in her brave way. I knew
there were no such things as ghosts
and that I was only dreaming, though later
I came to believe that dreams were stranger
than ghosts, and less earthly.
We went downtown to see the great hypnotist
at the concert hall, and I sat on my hands
when he told us to lock our fingers together.
My mother assured me you couldn't be hypnotized
unless you wanted to be, but I wasn't taking
any chances. How could I be sure what it was
I wanted, in my heart of hearts?
The girls down the street had learned to perform
levitation. They covered Cathy Murphy with a sheet
and touched the sides of her body lightly
with their fingertips until she rose into the air
like a loaf of bread, but Cathy made us promise
not to tell. Her mother would say
it was the work of the devil and beat her
with a wooden spoon, so we kept quiet.
I went home and listened to the minister on the radio,
the one who could cure arthritis and make
the blind to see, if they believed,
if they were in a state of grace.
If you touched the radio you could feel
the power of God, which my father called
static electricity because in our house
there were no such things as ghosts and no
magic. All of this was long before
any man ever loved me. These were just some
of the things I saw as I passed
through delusion and ignorance
and fear: those were the various
states of grace allowed to me
in my small life.

Paralysis

Sometimes in the middle of the night
or early in the morning, I would find myself
unable to move. Even my eyeballs were frozen
open, watching the crabapple branches
outside the window, my grandmother's dresser, books
and papers strewn across the floor.
If I could move one muscle, I'd be free.
There was another body inside my own body
struggling to escape, and sometimes I knew
I was wandering around inside my own chest,
inside my own head, seeking the way out, the light
that would pour in if only I could open
my mouth. I beat on that closed door
with my small fists, but nothing gave way.
In the garden, my mother tended the peonies
or my brother shovelled snow, and they moved
the same way I moved; I could feel them
in me sometimes as I lifted my elbow
from the table or turned a corner, shutting
a door with the heel of my left foot
just as they did. There was something
like an animal that lived inside us all,
divided but whole and more powerful
than we were and without a name.
At four o'clock in the morning, our father sat
in the purple chair in the living room
like Rodin's thinker, while I sneaked
past him toward the bookshelf.
In those days I believed he did not notice me,
but he was a trained boxer, a soldier, a man
who meditated nightly on the lessons of awareness.
There were the two of us, awake
while everyone else was sleeping.
He must have sensed a part of him
had slipped out of sleep, out of paralysis
and come down the fourteen stairs
looking for something to read, something
that would keep the mind alive
and moving, and outside of the body
where the danger was.

HVNGER

When one of us scraped a knee or stubbed a toe, our father
would ask, *why do you punish yourself like that?*
He was joking, I guess, though no one smiled.
Mr. Krentz, the history teacher, would smile
whenever he punished us. The boys said if you placed a hair
on your palm when he strapped you, he'd draw blood.
Then he'd catch it. He'd be sorry. But when the teachers
threatened me, I looked at them until they looked away.
If they ever try to make you sing the hymns, my father said,
you tell them you don't believe in that. You tell them
your father is God, he said, and he laughed.
In the detention room, Susan drew a picture of the teacher
with lips like the lips of a fish, and when we got caught,
I said I was hungry and ate it. I chewed and swallowed,
my eyes bright with tears. One of the problems we had
was that we never knew if our father was serious or not.
One of the problems we had was that I read too much.
I read Keats all afternoon and fell into a stupor.
I opened the refrigerator door and stood there,
staring in. *Whatever you're looking for,* my father said,
it's not in there. After work, some nights,
he was so tired he would fall asleep at dinner,
his head bowed on his chest, as if in prayer.
At six o'clock in the evening, every house
on the block was lit with warmth. I walked home
slowly, hearing the knives and forks chattering
through the screen doors. I made believe I was lost
and had no home. Outcast, I longed to be welcomed
to a stranger's table. Then I was late for dinner
and my father told me to get to my room.
Make me, I said, and he did. I sat on my bed
and looked at the shoes my father had paid for.
I looked at the depth of my ingratitude
for a minute. Then I climbed out the window
down the branches of the crabapple tree.

The playground was full of disobedient children.
Danny and Brian and Susan and me, all swinging
as high as we possibly could till the sun went down.
Danny dared me to jump, so I closed my eyes and waited
till the swing was near the top and then let go.
But even as I flew through the air, I knew I was still
inside my body with my family inside me. I bloodied
both my knees in the gravel, and then I punched Danny,
hard, in the stomach, and almost made him cry.
I wanted to know where my power had come from and when
it would take me completely. All the way home
I rubbed at my sore knuckles, wondering.
In the morning, my father was searching for something.
The drawers banged open and shut. A chair turned over.
I hoped some day the shell of my body would crack
right open and I would escape. In the meantime
I listened to my father as he looked for something
he could not find and wouldn't name for us.
Doesn't that just rot your socks, he said.
I waited for my inheritance.

DELIRIVM

I knew I was invincible the night I stole
away Mary Margaret's boyfriend
in the middle of winter, and Mary Margaret
let me. It seemed she was mesmerized
into a sorry acceptance of her lot.
She sat limp on the floor in the bathroom
during the dance, just cursing my eyes
and weeping, while I soaked up every latent
particle of sex and music and the whisky
that the boys had smuggled in
until there was a vacuum of power
in the room, an imbalance in the order of things.
I stood at the top of the bleachers
and called out his name, dared him to climb
through the trapdoor in the ceiling onto the roof
all because of his fine green eyes
and the way that Mary Margaret
had slighted me once, and it was easy.
It was twenty-two below and he followed me
with his eyes half open, as if he were sleep walking.
He seemed out of place up there on the roof
with the quarter moon lighting the snow clouds
over his head. He wasn't what I had expected
after all. So I released him. All night
the band played songs of longing and intoxication.
He danced with Mary Margaret twice, but a change
had come over them both for everyone to see.
They didn't seem ready to begin their lives.
She was delirious with anger, and he
was bewildered, a little like a patient
who had slipped out of the hospital
before he had been cured. That's how I learned
how easy it is to make a man feel
that you're not quite finished with him,
but someday you might be. Someday,
if you felt like it, you just might
finish him off.

Deliverance

I didn't recognize what he was giving to me,
he was a stranger, and he handed it over

so carelessly it might have been nothing at all,
just a switchblade casually laid

against my neck on Langside Street, 1975,
first lick of snow on the fallen

leaves, on the pink, amputated shoulder
and wing of a pigeon on the icy street—but wait

this isn't a story of trauma, a story
of silencing, failure, though it's true

I was young and slow to see what he was offering,
what he was telling me

just before my skin split, slightly
a small sound, like the parting of petals

and there it was: this generous
forcing open of things, this invitation to belong

I didn't know what I would say, exactly,
but I knew I was going to speak

it was going to be effortless
as tearing the wing from a little bird

the whole history of my short life swelled
inside me at last, at last

I was the one with the power
I was the one with the knife

to my throat, and I knew
I had always been dying

to tell these stories: how I became a girl
who would slice out your heart

as soon as look at you,
how I gained ascendance

over everyone

RVSH HOVR

this is the place where the five cars
collided in a long string as though
they were trying to become each other
the way you want to become your lover
as if it were possible to draw him through you
as you draw hot water through a sieve until
the water understands the sieve

but whatever water is, it is not
what we are; the five cars
sharp and hard, their steel
bodies breaking
through bone

this is the corner where the husband hunted down
his wife through the rush-hour traffic
she ran between the cars
and as she was running, her terror
beating through the city
like an awful drum, he cut her
and cut her and still
she continued to run

is this fate? this useless thing
that hangs like an unfinished sentence

can you call this thing by the name of death?

between your knees you hold the blue notebook
and your cheap, paperback copy of myths, a poor
translation, the covers closed, deliberately
as eyelids, over the words *hero, tragedy, fate*

when you were young and unemployed, the story
of Icarus moved you, you wept
right here on a bus on Portage Avenue, thinking,
irony, irony

thinking you knew this city

this sieve of a city

can you lift your eyes and look
at this corner, the ice-cream store, the park
with its footbridge and kites, the small ducks
circling the pond?

the moment has leaked into everything here,
the words *broad daylight, witnesses*

you heard there was one young man, a stranger
who stood above her desecrated body
with a shovel, protecting her
although she was already lifeless

and aren't they alive, if we believe
they are alive? from the window you think
you can see your friend Colette, her brown arms
swinging loose before her

then she is gone, nothing
there but the winter rain

was he afraid when he faced that madman of a husband?
did he believe himself immune to hunting knives?

these are questions you cannot ask because
she died

because he has returned
to his obscurity, his ordinary life

he returned suddenly, completely

you watch the chain of headlights
snaking through the dusk

you feel you could pick it up at one end and whip it
like a string of Christmas lights above your head

you are angry, you are angry

you are less than angry, you are just
a small, defeated thing

you stood at the bus depot
counting out your coins to buy a ticket
you were fifteen, you were leaving
this city, you were never
going to come back

you remember how that felt

but the streets pull you, they pull you
through them until you are made to understand

here you are, still, with your notebook
the book of myths half open and already
too well-read

this trade, you think,
is like the undertaker's trade:
to imagine here on the white sheet
the semblance of breath

the whole city lies before you
limp and flayed like a skinned fish

you are tired

they say there is a kind of beauty
among the children in the streets

the condoms and the bleached needles they clutch
like holy candles in their chapped hands

the names of their mothers and sisters
inked deep into their arms

you do not find this beautiful

Colette was beautiful
before she drowned

and the young wife, too

you are giving up
the search for beauty

you start to put your faith in giving up

it looks good to you

although you have passed the corner
where she bled to death in daylight
she is still with you

she is with all of us, she is
this long ride home
from the hospital, this city
you have never been able
to leave behind you

its twelve mighty bridges
its pigeons, its people
who skate on the rivers at night, gliding
over thin ice, eyelashes
dusted with frost

she is in every lamppost, every
crack in the cement

perhaps she believed she would escape

so many people, *broad daylight*
when she fell, when she was falling

you read that the young stranger
saw the garden shovel lying
in a neighbour's yard
and grabbed it up and ran
into the traffic

he claimed he did it without thinking

without thinking, this is the way
you want to live, now

your father once got lost near here, the white cane
useless in his hand as he forgot what year it was

the Nazi tanks were coming for him
through that blank and muddy space
between the trenches, a dream from which
he could never open those eyes

he told you many times, *there are no heroes*

he can only hear the city, he can only
feel his way along its haunted, rumbling streets

and haven't you felt it, too,
nights when the blue and white tower
of the CBC station seems to bow
before a power greater than the wind
and this thin strip of meat
we call the avenue twists and flips
like a ribbon come loose from a parcel

isn't it true that if Dedalus pinned
his waxed wings to the shoulders
of this city's wealthiest son
he would refuse to rise?

the tower persists
it is a great brain, a tall
electric brain, and its white,
                multiple eye
looks through you

when you sit with your notebook in some
coffee shop on Portage Avenue
and the rain comes down, the sirens
moan, the waitress leans her cheek
against the window

and for a moment both of you believe
you can hear the city breathing

you are both tired, you want to be done

at the corner of Portage and Main
you look up at the tall windowed
gods of your city
brooding over their vast holdings
and you start to believe
in the death of heroes

and that's when you need to remember
the young man with the shovel
how he offered up all that he owned:
his red veins for hers that were draining
his pumping heart for hers that was pierced
and had stopped; he stood
between the blade and the body
of this woman he had never known
he said, *this is the one thing here*
that is human; I will honour it

Drawing Water

at the Clear Lake museum my daughter writes
in the guest book, name and comments
she peers into the glassy eyes of lynxes
stuffed grouse, and bears, boring in death
if you stare long enough at the cougar
he will leap right through your heart and take you
with him to the afterlife of animals
when Terri and I were kids, we wrote in this book:

Mr. Bear. I came to visit my wife.

nothing to do but watch the pencil shavings
drift onto the dock and blow away, all day
the wind's been changing with the startling
swiftness of my daughter's moods
white clouds torn across the sun
the lake pale green and grey and impossibly
dense with the confidence of slate
as if I could pull this pencil across its surface

and then the rain begins

the art of recovering from pneumonia consists
of this: a lake, an electrical storm,
a long distance call during which the patient is told
take care of yourself, you belong to me
it consists also of a necessary amnesia:
finding in the morning after rain
every sketchbook left outside rinsed clean
of thought, and a kind of hunger

in the body when it wakes

my daughter's body, under the surface
of the pool, ripples and wrinkles
back into its first, tentative configuration
of cells, her underwater skin absorbing
vitamin D, the ultra-violet rays that spread
like a wavering halo from the brown fronds
of her hair, as if I were witnessing
the clear flow of her thoughts

into the world

convalescence: a thin sheen of fever
peeling from the skin like cellophane
lungs expanding in their glass cage:
breath, a love of elementary things again
the taste of bread and apples
even the lake, in its cold mutability,
touches the tongue
I belong to you: what's that?

some kind of metaphor?

even the soft, rag pages of the sketchbook
cannot absorb this light, the crystallized webs
suspended in the morning grass, the braided streams
of water from the outdoor tap
the boys in their rowboat
call to my daughter, "Hey,
girl in the red—girl in the red shirt—"
everything already dappled with memory loss

like the uneven pigment under my skin

the arguing crows on the rooftop pause
for a second, and one of them suddenly
darts his beak toward the other, caresses
the glossed black feathers
as though tempted, inexplicably
by human love, and then he flies away
above the cedar trees, and this small incident
seems to inform the day, the children on the beach

their dance with the dangerous waves

cigarette ashes fall on the page
and only the lightest of breaths
will clear them away without smudging
the drawing of water, the day
full of surprises, the pain returning
suddenly under the left lung
steel blade of speechlessness
just a reminder: light is temporary

it sharpens itself on the eye, grows thin

from the edge of the dock we watch the sun set
above the forest on the far shore of the lake
and the burning clouds are whipped by the wind
into temple spires, prison towers, the sky
a vast city on fire, site of a holy war
as evening eases in, the bombed-out shells
of neighbouring villages glow
and are extinguished

we both see the same impossible thing

I dream the sharp mouth of the lynx
and wake, afraid to finish the sentence
the lake air enters the left ventricle
from the north, settles in the alveolus
and condenses there, invisible, untouched
by the sun that burnishes clouds into cities
little chance, now, that the pencil will ever
render water, or the crows, the beautiful daughter,

the bear in her predatory stance, beckoning

across the telephone lines, small silences
between each word, your voice, recorded,
repeating the story of your absence, lost quarters
perhaps this pain is human and will talk to me
after all, it is part of the body
or seems to be, and if only the light would cease
to skim like that across the surface
of the sky, if only the birds on the lake

this is the language of water, muted

I only wanted to say I know full well
that crows do not yield so easily
to understanding, nor will my daughter's thoughts
ever unravel before me, but even in this long
intractable summer of water and sunlight,
the world seems to give up
its hiddenness; it surrenders
in certain illusory, irresistible moments:

an ant crawling over the drawing
of an ant I've made on the page

Ghost Stories

I

the morning my husband called me to the window
and said *look*, I looked, and we saw a man
walking backwards, barefoot in the snow

these are the signs of loss: the red mitten perched
on the hood of a parking meter, ice
clinging to the wool like beads of sweat

the mitten thumbtacked to the bulletin board

the white diamonds of a chain-link fence
in a blizzard, every wire hung with frost
and on top of the fence-post, a mitten

those times when you stand on your front porch,
keys in your hand
am I leaving something behind?

or halfway down the stairs,
the reason for descending
suddenly escapes you

the way the meaning of a word disintegrates
with repetition

the way the snow obliterates beauty
with beauty, *un trou de mémoire*
white flakes swirling
in the black hole

how we commiserate with one another:

I arrived at the station without a ticket
at the marketplace without my purse
without my parcel my pencil my green umbrella
that's nothing,
                I locked myself out,
let my wedding ring
glide down the drain, stepped
on the gas instead of the brake
                that's nothing
left the briefcase on the bus, the pot on the stove
the water running, left my fiddle
on the roof of the car and drove away
it slid like a sled down Portage Avenue

that's nothing

3

the night I climbed the wooden ladder down from my bed
in the darkness, there at the kitchen table
a strange man sat with his great knees drawn up
toward his chin, head in his hands,
as though he were simply bewildered

I remembered a book I was reading
about the spirit, how it is sometimes
reluctant, recalcitrant as a child
on the way to school in the winter time,
lingering, leaving a thin trail
of belongings in its wake

look at the branches, burdened
with silver shadows, the colourless sky,
the wind that sways the telephone wires
until they shed their thick white pelts

he was holding his head in his hands
he was wearing a work shirt, over-alls, I believe
he was lost, somehow he had stumbled
into the wrong house, a mistake
any one of us might make

4

breathe on the frosted pane,
the heavy tapestry of vegetation, white

you can see your breath, because winter makes visible
what ought not to be visible

and they say that in latitudes north of the Arctic circle
you can tell when someone has crossed your path
so cold that the body leaves a body-shaped hole
behind it when it moves, a temporary
corridor through the white air

still, it is snowing

5

what else is there
to a ghost story?

simply our fear

that we won't die

entirely

the light will still see us
we won't be completely transparent
there will always be something
we have neglected to do

6

and you, what do you think you are doing
coming toward me, late
as usual and carrying nothing

slowly, as if the air
that surrounds you
had grown heavy, tired
with the weight of you

the way I grew tired, waiting

7

you returned to me
the gloves I had left in the post office
the black ones, with the small
hole in the left thumb
de rien, you said, *we are all of us*
forgetful, distracted

you told me you never could finish
anything, money burned a hole
in your pockets, you misplaced things
they would slide from your grasp, slick
as polished ice

these were your faults, you said
you enumerated them for me

8

as for myself, I am always forgetting
what it was I wasn't going to write about
what I wasn't going to say again

that it was snowing, you walked out
into the street without looking, you left me behind

and it was easy, it was nothing
the cold air so thin you could slip right into it
the way a dime will slip into a snowbank, leaving
no trace
          although we are all of us returning
and returning to the place
where it went missing

coming back again, the wind stilled for a moment
in the branches, holding its breath,
absent-minded, the way we are all of us absent-minded,
the way we forgive ourselves our lapses,
so suddenly, swiftly, without any effort at all
we let our two lips part
to tell our stories

Latent Heat

Seven Arteries

Four o'clock in the morning
and the man on the radio
says, *there are seven arteries*
of prayer, there are seven
parts to a man's heart, and then
because it is early summer, light
edges the curtains, and I turn,
unable to find sleep again.

The snow falls; isn't it true
that I am always saying that? But
it falls, it drifts, it buries
the garden where the tulips poke their red tips
through the earth too early. It buries
the house, the bed, the radio, the voice
of the man who was telling me
to open my veins for Jesus, and you
will not appear in my thoughts
this morning. I will not speak of you.

A yellow bird my daughter fashioned
out of paper with her small hands twirls
on its string in the window, and the snow falls
through the seven levels of the city:
white airplane streaks across the sky,
the telephone wires, bridges, avenues, the pipes
shot through with gas and water, the dead
with gold rings on their skinny fingers,
their hair still growing underground.
It might be possible to raise the layers
of this city and lay them down again, ever so
gently, the way you lift a sheet above the bed
and let it drift down slowly without wrinkles, or
the way you leaf through your anatomy textbook
backwards and then forwards, watching
the transparent woman wax
and wane: muscle, marrow, nerve
and finally skin that we can peel away
as simply as we lift a piece of paper.

Now the man on the radio begins a song
about cleansing the soul in blood, and all I want
is to escape this web of consciousness, to burrow
into one of those dreams of falling, darker
than heroin, deeper than sleep. But there is never
anything here except the same stupid surprise:
the way I will open myself to you
again and again.

Unexpectedly, without warning, I will step
through this hole and come undone,
the seven arteries unravelling, the delicate,
coloured wires coming loose; I will unfold
into the darkness like one of those ignorant
flower bulbs, and you will look at me
the way a doctor looks at a patient
he's about to open. He imagines the seven parts
of the heart and their location under the skin.
He thinks of the dead, how they peel themselves bare
when no one's looking, revealing the strange
white roots of the body. They lie
beneath the city, breathless, waiting
for resurrection. They can hear the distant singing
on the Sunday radio. They hear
our footsteps, up above them
in the early summer snow.

The Seventh Day *

the first grey feather of smoke
came drifting from the sky too soon
too early, my work still left undone
the golden world gone dry and catching
fire on the east horizon, with me still
holding its glory in my mouth, about to speak
and when my spine broke, when the flames came singing
through me then I saw it all, the whole combustible
beauty, the black cut blades of grass and wings
the colour of rust, the colour of dark frost
burnt flowers like coal, like dull silver
how I could have spoken everything, there
on the parapet I was giving in at last I was going
down in ecstasy, folding my paper hands
beneath my paper face, forgetting the story
of what I could have made if I had not
so easily let go

* after seeing Esther Warkov's *Word Warrior*

The Other Side

they say if the hairs on your arm begin to rise
you're about to be struck by lightning

they say the human body is an intricate machine
you study Michelangelo, da Vinci,

run the tip of your pencil lightly
over your wrist bone, over your thumb

you still can't see below the skin
you look up the heart in an old biology textbook

copy the diagram into your notes
watch the sky crack open

tell the children thunder is nothing
but noise

they say when a ghost walks into a room,
the air grows tangible and quivers

the way the heart
begins to tremble before love

or inspiration, any visit
from the other side

is this how it happens?
sheer surrender

the oak tree lifts its limbs
as though relieved of gravity

every green leaf rises
separate and expectant

the white blue line
descends

The Windowsill

1

a tiger lily, two yellow candles
pens and pencils in a coffee tin

a wine bottle holds the window open
and a breeze comes in, the sound of sparrows

this is the place where a pregnant woman
writes about love, early in the morning

she tiptoes to the windowsill, not wanting
to wake the children

the lily has opened like a hand
revealing its clean black freckles

the bright flame of its pistil, stamens
that tremble toward the rising sun

the woman describes the one she loves
carefully, completely

she leaves out nothing

2

the carpenter understands about the space
between the inside and the outside

how the sun can pour
right through a pane of glass

and travel through the veins the way a child
will travel through its mother

he knows this is the place
where women water their flowers

where words rise in their throats
before the day begins

therefore he chooses the wood with care
he sings while he works

he draws the plane across the board
dark wood flakes curl

like petals to the floor

3

you see, I was writing this note to you
about labour and devotion

a lily that opened like fire and gold
a man who turned his face up toward the sun

I wanted to tell you how silent it was
in the morning and how lonely

the sparrows were singing, a breeze
came in at the window

I thought about leaving my work
and going out to look for you

the way a woman will lift up her head
from the page when the children wake

the way she will describe the light
by leaving her notebook open

on the windowsill

The Letter L

it is a sound that moves
across the garden in the morning
soaking the dark stones with light
it is a long sound, a sound you can run
through your fingers like water, like
silk, it is the sound the lily speaks
when it finally opens, hesitant,
the way that a man who has suffered
a stroke is hesitant; his mouth
will open and close without stopping
his tongue touching his upper teeth
as though he is saying a word

this is the most liquid letter, the silver
one, the one that slips out of the body
like a newborn cat, it is the one with the wide
loops and you are drawing it over and over
waiting for the word; is it loss,
holding you here in the hospital room
is it longing or love or maybe
he is telling you to let go,
let go, the lily begins to fold itself up
for the evening, and still he has not spoken

The Movie

for Jack

it was another story of rescue, the same damned
helpless woman and the car chase and the villain
and the hero, so why was I sobbing, yes,
that was my shame, watching the young man
race across the city like an animal,
his young, young, beautiful face
completely in the moment, throwing his body
on the woman, his most excellent, sturdy arms around her
the two of them rolling together, out of the flare
of the explosion, out of death, and I felt my face
contorting in the darkness of the theatre
there it was again: that most secret passion,
not for sex or fame or even shelter, but for simple
clarity, a single glass where you can see yourself,
your whole life there before you, sharp and clean
as something that could cut you and you run,
you know where to run, you reach out
and take it

13 Lines in Order to Forget You

a scientist draws a picture of the brain
on the blackboard, she labels the memory
with a piece of chalk

a doctor raises his hand, a question
flutters on the tip of his tongue
what were we talking about again?

meanwhile, a patient with amnesia wanders
down the hall and walks out of the hospital
how easily you've slipped my mind

I have forgotten you, and
if I were the two-headed woman
on the cover of the *National Enquirer* today

I would forget you twice

The Twenty-sixth

for George and for George

You got hurt in September, or almost
September—it was August twenty-sixth,
the buckets of chokecherries already full
of wasps, the silver maples sending their
white seeds flying through the neighbourhood,
the evening star becoming unreliable.
You knew this was not just any summer
you were losing. You knew this was serious.
You ached. You stood in the garden and counted
eighty-seven green tomatoes. How
could you possibly ease their ripening?

Your friend, a brilliant poet, writes from Mexico,
asking why it is you set such value
on these foolish things. What is the matter
with you? You are becoming repetitive
and intellectually lazy and what's worse
you know it yourself. Still, September, or
the coming of September, hurt you.

The twenty-sixth of August was a treacherous day.
It was there and yet it was not there.
Oh dangerous summer of 1997! You were attached
to the evening star, the chokecherries, even
the wasps, the cat with her one blind eye,
a certain stubborn man who will not
fix your bicycle. Still you are attached to him!
What is the matter with you anyway?
You are attached to the eighty-seven
green tomatoes, every unripe one of them.

JANVARY

Nine children in the house on a winter morning,
cats and too much music and a slow leak in the water heater.

You pick up the three coins you found when you cleaned
the heat exchange and consult the I Ching.

What does one thing have to do with another?
Sometimes you sense a current in the air

that seems to bind things together, but this morning
it is ephemeral, barely perceptible.

January, January, you walk through the house
repeating the name of the month like a mantra.

It does not enlighten you. And the Book of Changes
speaks only of *fire over wood* and whether *it furthers one*

to cross the great water, nothing relevant to your life.
Ah, your life, here in this city of winter,

this winter of winters, broken glass under ice
and white light coming in at the window.

Sometimes you believe you might begin to weep
but what would you weep for? There is nothing

particularly sad here, the children are content.
They carry every blanket down from the bedroom

and make themselves a refuge under the table.
The cats sleep, as they always sleep, through January.

You need to clear a space out of this absence
that surrounds you, a place where absence

is absent, a place from which departure has gone.
But the day comes loose from its hinges,

unfastens itself while you are not looking,
and like all winter days, closes too soon

and yet remains open. Its gaps fill up with snow.
What belongs to you here? You have forgotten

to lay claim to anything, even the names
of the children, the names of the cats,

the name of this particular symphony by Mozart,
a man who never knew these winters

the way you do, or thought you did, for now
even the name of the season escapes you.

The *Book of Changes* lies open on the table,
leaking words, and the children are hungry.

Perhaps this is what you have been waiting for,
the process of cooking and eating, a false warmth

in the afternoon while the dull white sun ascends
to a low point in the sky, begins to sink again.

You sluice the cast iron pan with oil
and break a dozen eggs, while the cats stir a little

in their hiding places, and Mozart rises
to a wild crescendo. You begin to remember

a slow brown river and the twelve bridges that span it,
a man who left and promised to return,

the way the coreopsis bloomed and bent
its thin stems in the wind,

the way your thoughts once had the power
to tie the various objects in this house together.

Navigation

All the way down—that's the most likely direction.
This is what you're thinking as you speed across the water,
the lake black as the islands that must be here—
they were here this afternoon. Now they have slipped
into this pool of a night, all trees and birds and rocks
submerged, the water darker than the sky, and deeper.

When you set your compass, you were unprepared for this.
You thought only north, west, south. You thought
east, the place from which the light arrives.
All day you took in nothing but plums and tequila, the sun
filled up your mouth, you were weightless, transparent,
ignorant of where you were about to travel.

You should have read the signs: those hands, those long
and muscled arms that drew you forward and let loose
the ropes, but you were sick of reading, sick of paper,
flight plans, calendars, marine charts.
You used to know a woman who wrote letters to the moon.
How far away she seems now, and how solitary.

Here, there are a thousand polar stars, the world a gap
of sky, the wind a sweet pain blowing through the space
that was your body. But surely this could not be death.
You are somewhere else entirely, a place without alibi.
You could say your instruments had been disabled
by those hands, the way they touched you

and unknotted you at last. Or you could say
it was lightning. You could say, very slowly,
the shoreline is a sentence without meaning.
When you were a child, you knew what falling was.
Now you are illiterate, you are forgetting
how you once distinguished one word from another.

How did it happen, this disaster, this eclipse, a storm
escaping the barometer? What will you think of
in these final moments, going down? Only that
there were no signs, unless you want to count
the memory of a kiss in which you once became
unutterably lost, and could not find your way again.

Elsewhere

Even when your face is turned
away from my eyes, I can still see you.
Even when you rise, you are still here
beside me, and believe me,
there is nothing you can do about this.
You have been split and rendered
timeless, inexhaustible, manifold,
a person in a painting by Duchamp.

And come December, when all distances
become impossible, you will be powerless
to stop these other versions
of yourself from sliding
through the winter streets
and entering my door.
Perhaps you will believe that you are sleeping.
This is one of those recurring dreams, or
you are growing thinner. You will never open up
this book and read what's here
for anyone to see: that love is a shredding.
It is a pool in which you will dissolve.

Before I ever saw you I was practising
these arts without a purpose, making words
without a single doubt about their tendency
to multiply, but now even when you're elsewhere,
the muscles of your arms at rest
and half lit in the early morning
of some other house, your jacket
hanging crooked and relieved
of you in someone else's closet—

Sometimes I look at other things: the war
on television, or a book review
in which the critic claims
the poem is single-minded, or the snow,
the snow. Sometimes I look
at the snow. It's white. I will not mention
the moon, a lyrical movement that might
be misconstrued as lust, or wistfulness.
I will return instead to you, for love
is a place where you are always with me.
You are here right now, or one of you
is here, looking tenderly across my shoulder
as I write you.

The First Lesson

for Heather

The first lesson is the easiest one
to forget: All things, very gradually,
will turn into themselves and disappear
from sight. Even this bright garden
of beets and flowers, this heat
and wind, these two human bodies,
how substantial they seem, how full
of suffering—hey! Those are *our*
bodies! We sit cross-legged,
pulling up grass blades, surrounded
by marigolds, early mushrooms, packages
of cigarettes. We are listening
to our daughters practise clarinet
and sax. They play by the open window
in the blue kitchen with its blue chairs, glass
vase of violets on the blue tablecloth.
They are making music while we count
for each other the many times we have been hurt.
Why am I here? you ask, and I give
my usual answer: *beets and mushrooms,*
dandelion seeds. I say, *wind instruments,*
and the smoke from our cigarettes rises
over my voice and dissipates like birds
in winter. Like a friend who comes and asks
a question and departs, leaving behind
in this small house her hairbrush
and a conversation that continues
when she's gone. And now if you were here
you'd see the places where we talked
swept over with a film of snow. Both of us
erased. If you were here you'd see
how I repeat myself, naming marigolds
and violets and a kitchen
where one summer afternoon the light
turned everything blue—but even these
are the wrong answers, useless
as cigarettes, useless as love
when it comes to what we really want,
the garden again, grief.

The Naked Eye

in memoriam, HJB

You are so far away, or let's be truthful,
you've been dead for twenty years,
a synapse in the brain of the city,
these streets so fractured, full of spaces.
I thought I saw you again this morning,
walking the maze of paths behind the planetarium,
as if you remembered the time
the teachers took us up there,
let us read the sky. They told us any loss
of matter is converted into energy. They gave us
metaphors: You disappeared
at the speed of light. They gave us telescopes.
But some things are apparent only
to the naked eye. I can stand
on the Norwood Bridge and seem to touch
the potent circuit of the river. Venus, small
as the spurt of a penny match, appears
suspended, caught in the gap
of the St. Boniface cathedral's
excoriated window frame. The downtown lights
are sparks the city lets go, attempting
to purify itself. This city is still hot,
young friend, white hot.
It runs on the electricity conducted
through the streets when heroes
turn to constellations.
It's heat that separates the metal
from the ore, because in metallurgy,
as in death, beauty smoulders closer
and closer to the surface
of the body, becoming visible at last,
setting itself free. The burnt cathedral,
with its empty window open like a mouth,
says, *ah.* The sound of finding
what it's lost. If you can see me,
make some sign. Darkness
is settling down, all over the suburbs,
and Venus is rising. I can almost see
the passion that set her blazing like a flare,
an SOS, a way of saying, *don't stop looking*
for me. I am here.

Fainting

The day she tells me about the shadow
on her lung, it is raining. We are eating
Italian salads in a new restaurant
on Sargent Avenue, and the rain comes down.
It seems it has been raining since winter.
It has always been raining, but we are not
thinking about that; we are having
a sort of conversation.

When she tells me about the biopsy, I begin
to yawn, I cannot stop yawning
and have to excuse myself, politely,
enter the bathroom, lie down
deliberately on the damp, ceramic floor, completely
unfit for this world, completely unready.

I remember the summer I was fourteen,
walking home alone through the baseball field
after the accident, looking at my hands.
I had been holding Kenny Robinson
in my arms until the ambulance came.
I sat on a park bench, his small,
split-open head in my lap, tugging
the loose flaps of flesh together.
And what I wasn't prepared for
was the thickness of his blood,
the way it stiffened on my skin like
candle wax, like egg yolk, the way it glued
my fingers together and afterwards, walking home I saw
the bleachers waver and blur, the horizon turn to ash.
The whole field drained of colour, and I sank
into the cool grass, losing entirely this thing
we call consciousness. It was a little death, I guess,
a little practice.

When I get enough oxygen into my brain, I lift my cheek
from the cold tiles of the bathroom floor and stand,
still pale but level-headed, adult, ready to return
to the restaurant, the rain, the Italian salad,
this woman I don't want to love anymore.
Already I can see her receding before me
the way that Kenny Robinson receded, sailing off
down a long tunnel toward a place I've never been,
a place where nobody can touch you,
nobody holds your head, you can't faint.
You just have to sit here eating lemons and cilantro,
asking about health insurance, who will take care
of the children, while the air grows warm and slightly sticky.
Neither of you were expecting this
heat, this viscosity. The rain comes down.
It is always raining. Whether you're conscious
or not, the streets are always
filling up with rain.

For God So Loved the World

Sometimes atheists secretly
roll the word *consecrated*
over their tongues. Sometimes
the world seems, ultimately, worthy
of love. Like today, snow melting
at the base of the elm tree, a hyacinth.
And that's not all—there is also
the sweater that Shirl is knitting
for David, coarse, articulate patterns,
white on white. There is the way Ron rescued
the silver ring your daughter gave you
from the river, plucking it, just like that,
from the perilous place it had fallen to
between the slivered planks of the dock.
There are the glasses that let you see.
You can read! You could read the bible,
but you don't. Atheists, too,
have their crises of faith. They're tempted,
like everyone else, by miracles: snow
and the melting of snow. Birds.
Every Easter, the bells ring early
through St. Boniface. New clothing.
You look at your sleeping child
and feel sorry for God. The sacrifice
he had to make. And to whom? What unimaginable being
could have demanded that terrible bargain
from the Holy Father? *That's* the one
we should be praying to. A Manitoba crocus
pushes its green leaves through the cold soil
in a single night, its white and purple flower
too delicate for such a world. Spare us.

Opening

Finally, the crazy lady moved out
of the neighbourhood. For years she stalked
this sidewalk with her fists clenched
tight as walnuts in the sleeves
of her unravelled cardigan and talked to birds
who were not there. Children would not answer
when she called them. At summer's end,
I harvest basil for the winter sauces.
When I crush the fragrant leaves
between my fingers and inhale, I can't help
thinking that I used to press your shirts
against my face like this.
Religion is a crutch, Jim always said,
but if you need it—hey, why not?
I pack the basil leaves in salt. I touch them
tenderly, I do not want to bruise them
any more. The crazy lady walked the way
the dead walk, listing. The neighbours,
as they always do, had theories:
she collided with a speeding truck
outside the abattoir, or else her heart
was fractured by a deep betrayal. In any case
she had been ripped wide open or perhaps
a hole had opened in the world
and she stepped through it.
When the children were too cruel, their mothers
scolded softly, using the crazy lady
as a way to teach gentility. They said,
she's only lonely. None of us admitted
that she told the truth. She'd wait beside
the mailbox for me and cry out: *I know
you are avoiding me! I see you!* Loss
is a series of simple things. Your shirts.
The basil plants. The crazy lady
who we loved, though she embarrassed us.
We had grown used to her. She was like a ghost
no one believed in anymore. She talked and talked
and filled the empty spaces of the neighbourhood.
Now she's gone and no one has replaced her,
yet. No one here is qualified to give us
what she gave us: something breakable and fierce
we could ignore.

Experts

for Patty

All day the experts fill the airwaves
with advice, and I am listening,
the volume turned up high to mask
the pounding of these typewriter keys.
Outside, Gwen is looking at my dandelions.
Norm is measuring the rotten step
on the back porch. Once I heard Trish say
that educated people lack the sense
to hammer in a nail. I spend an hour
searching through the books stacked
three feet high above the stove, wanting
only one quotation about glass. The man
from city hall's convinced the elm tree
must be pruned. He says that sacrifice
is vital to survival, so I keep on typing
while the expert on the radio is listening
with impatience to the tales of women callers
who cannot control themselves. They sleep
with gamblers, convicts, men
of little faith. Gwen claims it's unlikely
she can rid this lawn of weeds without
some kind of poison, and the expert
on the radio says crisply, once again,
that love is not enough. I can't tell you
how untouched I am by all of this.
I'm hearing only what the women's hearts
are singing. Underneath my breath I hear them
chant: *of course it is enough,*
of course it is, of course. And then tonight
the poet from across the street appears
beneath my window, two quart bottles
of homemade beer in his hands.
He asks, "do you remember my line,
that line from the other night
about the darkness?" Behind his head
the stars are caught in the clouds
and the clouds are caught in the branches
of the elm.

Mess

I used to think the word
metaphysical had something to do
with minerals—the hardness of diamonds,
crustacean fossils in the limestone
on the Legislature steps. That was when
words were obvious, lit from within
by the clear intelligence of sound.
This morning, the house seems burdened
with gratuitous objects. The sticky dishes
from our pancakes, seven
hundred books, the china cup our cat
was drinking from before she died.
As always, George's pipe tobacco
in its smelly case. And on the wall,
a purple poster from the art gallery:
Catherine Collins' "Little Eden,"
a portrait of the Central Laundry
on Cumberland Street, abandoned,
every painful picket of its white fence
rendered bare. My neighbourhood, too,
is littered with unnecessary detail.
The solid bodies of pigeons, shivering
under the bridge. Bulldozers, brick,
the whole disastrous
conglomeration of matter—Jack riding by
on his bicycle with the day's finds,
a discarded guitar balanced, teetering,
on his handlebars. Transcendence
sounds so easy, painless, the body's
molecules coming loose like salt
dissolved in water. This afternoon
when Annie phoned long distance
and said her hotel room was fifty floors
above the street, I felt the coiled cord
of my telephone become a kite string, holding
her up there, barely attached to this world

of clutter, and I was afraid
to let go. Sometimes I suspect I have mistaken
the meaning of every word. I think
I should leave the reading and writing
to others. I should tidy up this place.
And then, in the yard, my three
childhood friends, or the memory of them,
gather, laughing in the evening rain.
I watch them through the roses
of the threadbare curtains. At night
we turn out all the lamps, and the dust,
the dirty dishes and the pipe tobacco
disappear. Only the white fence
in the Catherine Collins painting gleams
in the dim room, because Catherine loves
this metaphysical city, her city, with its real
buildings, its real mess. I want to whisper
to every invisible thing in the house,
the way a man once whispered to me
in the darkness, "don't
ever leave me. Stay close."

Gifted

I looked up the word *recalescence*
in the dictionary and then became
distracted. I was thinking of the way
that lovers kiss on February streets.
At twenty-nine below they open up
their mouths and breathe each other.
The geese who fly across the lake
have seen the secret core of winter.
The mailman is on strike, but every day
at noon I still look out the window.
You could say procrastination is a gift,
a kind of talent. Outside, the carnations
buried in their overcoats of snow
remember nakedness. Dinah Washington
is singing "Say it isn't so."
Open the dictionary—
recalescence: *a brightening*
exhibited by cooling iron as the latent heat
of transformation becomes liberated.
I am waiting for you.
You could say it is an art form
I'm attempting
to perfect.

TRVE NORTH

When I close my eyes I can still see the light
on the surface of the Winnipeg River, the five orphaned ducks
and the white wings of the pelicans lifting beyond
any conception of flight, or water. What is memory
that it lives like this beneath the skin
of the eyes? The pelicans lifted their wings
and measured the distance between north
and true north. I peeled back the tough,
cellulose coat of a water lily, held in my palm
the fat gold seeds in their white, gelatinous casing.
I wanted to say to you: Nothing passes.
Nothing passes away. Not even the fires you lit
at night when the other world seemed so close at hand.
Sparks licked at the grasses, and Jupiter described
the slow rotation of Earth. Sometimes we spoke
of those who had left us, and sometimes we were silent.
I thought of Shelley, how he believed his words
would circle the globe, set it aflame, and then he drowned.
I thought of the sun, how its indelible heat still marked
your body in the darkness as you slept. Meanwhile,
the crazed dog at the end of the dock could not stop
diving and diving into the river. What is the direction
of desire? Simply up through the green, shot stem
of the lily, straight into the middle of things.
Soon, we will all be travelling there, willing
or no. And if I go first, I'll measure the distance
for you. I will leave behind few words
to mark the passage, for it will be necessary only
to say this: white wings of the pelicans
lifting the light on the river a fire that will not
ever burn away a summer night when we were all alone
and the world pretended, momentarily, to give us
what we asked of it.